POETIC & RELIGIOUSLY
Beautiful

RICHARD L. ALLEN

PUBLISHED BY FIDELI PUBLISHING INC.

Copyright 2014, Richard L. Allen

All rights reserved.

No part of this book may be reproduced or shared by any electronic or mechanical means, including but not limited to printing, file sharing, and email, without prior written permission from Fideli Publishing.

ISBN: 978-1-60414-758-2

Mission Statement

My poetry is intended for all GOD fearing and loving poetry readers. It's a statement intended to reveal how I feel and think about some things, how some thought out things may have become thoughtfully poetic and religiously beautiful.

Other poetic works from this God-fearing author:

Lock And Key

A New Ark Police Officer's View Of Just Ice / Justice

Poetic Police Food For Thought

Poetic Black

The All About Children / Kids Book

Poetic Black II

Kindergartners On Their First School Bus

Cool To Be In School

Picture Book for Christian Kids

All of the above books are available on Amazon.com and other online retailers.

Table of Contents

Hope 1
Thanks 2
Love 3
Glory Glorifying Gloriously 4
Faith 5
Jehovah God 6-7
King 8
Love One Another 9
Church 10
Soul 11
Christian Christians 12
Holy One 13
The Holy Ghost 14
A Rainbow 15
A Wedding 16
Cinderella 17
Try, Try, Try Me 18
Exalted 20
Tarried 21
Ascend Above Our Descend 22
Hallelujah 23
Almighty 24
Saved 25
Sabbath 26
Sepulchure 27
Believers 28

Straightway	29
Hilltops	30
Drug Addicts	31
He	32
POWA	33
Truth	34
God	35
Live or Die Lord	36
A True Living God	37
Our Salvation	37
Victory	39
I Love You	40
Heart	41

HOPE

```
        H
        O
HO      PE
        P
        E
```

Heaven is
Open for
People, who are
Eager to live forever as *Christians*.

Hope can become

One's staircase to

Permanent peace, an

Everlasting and very happy life.

Heaven is waiting with
Open arms for those who
Prefer to enter, opposed to
Entering elsewhere.

Richard L. Allen

```
     T
     H
THANKS
     N
     K
     S
```

Many Thanks for giving
And Thanks
Dear Lord
For giving
Us another chance
To live forever.
Many Thanks
For Thanksgiving
And all the giving
From *You,*
That's being
And been
Offered our way.
Please *Dear Lord*
Accept these many Thanks
From all of us,
That's been
And being
Offered *Your Way.*

Poetic & Religiously Beautiful

```
    L
    O
LOVE
    V
    E
```

To love
And to be loved
Is a very lovely
Feeling.
To lovingly
Feel
All over
Are the feelings
Felt
When love exhales
And excels
Its very special warmth. To love
And to become loveable
Is catching
And getting caught
Up in loving
Feelings,
While displaying our own love
And loving
Feelings
For **The One Who Loved Us First.**

Richard L. Allen

Glory
Christians must allow
Their lively
And lifeline
Ribbons
To always fly high and

Gloriously
Honoring Our Lord,

Glorifying
His Existence, with all

Glory
Added to *His Name*,
Glorification
Streaming from *His Name*,
Glorious

Is to see
And say
His Holy Name

Glories,
Glorify,

Honor
And All Praises
To His Heavenly Name.

Glories,

Glorify,

Honor
And All Praises
To His Heavenly Name.

Poetic & Religiously Beautiful

```
    F
    A
  FAITH
    T
    H
```

Our true faith
In Our Dear God
And Lord
Makes any waiting
For any help
Worthwhile,
Worth the wait,
Worth its weight,
In desired goals,
Less prolonged
With the ending results
Longed-for.

Our true faith
Makes our needs
More able to comprehend,
Rewarding,
When they are rewarded
Heavenly
And hoped for faithfully,
Because of our
Or any hour
Of true faith
In *Our Dear Lord*
And God.

Richard L. Allen

```
        J
        E
      GHG
   JEHOVAH
      DVD
        A
        H
```

Our Lord, God, The Messiah, Our Father,
Christ, Jesus, I Am, The Prince of Peace,
Master, King, Allah, Our Savior,
Son Of Man and Jehovah.

His many
Holy names
Are as divine
And *Holy*
As *He* is.

Although
His
Divinity
Is The One
Truth
And Trueness
In any form
Of interpretation.

Poetic & Religiously Beautiful

Just as our air
Is true
To all life forms
And another true gift
Aired
From **God.**

The truest gift
Is allowing us to become heirs
To share **His**
Heavenly Kingdom.

Richard L. Allen

```
        K
        I
K I     N   G
        N
        G
```

Our Dear Lord God Is The Supreme King of all

Kings, *He's* our
Innovator of love
Narrator of life
God of all and is truly *The Greatest King* above all else.

My and your **K**ing
        Is King
        Now, King,
        God and Lord forever.

Thank You, Dear Lord, for Being the

Kind and merciful
Illustrator of the
New world to come, also for the
Greatness, goodness and graciousness awaiting therein.

Poetic & Religiously Beautiful

LOVE
ANOTHER
E

Love everyone,

Obey our hearts,

Vent our love and

Expand loving thoughts

> One step at a time
> Now and
> Everyday.

> > Another moment should
> >
> > Not pass
> >
> > On or by
> >
> > This day, when our
> >
> > Hearts didn't
> >
> > Extricate loving
> >
> > Respect for each other.

Richard L. Allen

```
        C
        H
        U
CHU     RCH
        R
        C
        H
```

           Our Church Homes are in our
                        e
Church   a
Goers   r
Should go   t
To *Church*   s
More often,
Without leaving
One's abode.
Particularly by looking
Into and searching
Our hearts,
In a *Christian*
Like effort
To re-visit
Our personal,
Integral *Church Homes*
On a daily
And more meaningful basis.

Poetic & Religiously Beautiful

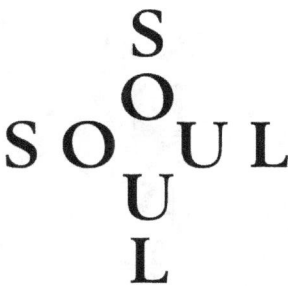

We must become keenly aware
And/or beware
Of **The One**
Who can
Destroy both life
And soul
In permanent fire.
We must not
Concern
Ourselves
With anyone,
Who can
Destroy just a life.
A keen interest of discern
Should be the necessary awareness,
Making us aware
Of who
We want to determine where
Our

    Surely
    Our one
    Underlining
    Life

Will live on, forever.

Richard L. Allen

```
        C
        H
        R
        I
CHRISTIAN
        T
        I
        A
        N
        S
```

Christ's children should be *Christ* **like in all of their**
Honorable endeavors,
Religious beliefs, other
Important
Social issues and
Tasks, including tongue control,
Inspirations,
Anger management,
Needs and
Snap reasoning.

Poetic & Religiously Beautiful

HOLY
N
E

Our Holy One, who resides in the most
Upper
Room in His Blessed Heaven, please

Listen to and grant
Our prayer
Requests. Please continue to
Deliver us from all inappropriate

Actions and intentions. Please continue to protect us
Night and day from
Dreadful criminal elements. Thank You for Your

Goodness and graciousness, over and above
Our imaginations; also for the Love from our most
Devine Being ever.

Richard L. Allen

THE HOLY

GHOST

The Holy Ghost

Will keep us from becoming lost
Amid a lifetime of fogginess. If we allow it to host
Our minds, at whatever the cost.
During our unforeseen tribulations is when we will need
It most.
Post
The Holy Ghost
All about, to prevent the likelihood of us becoming
Redundant toast
In a permanent place of fire
And ire.

Poetic & Religiously Beautiful

<pre>
      A
      R
      A
      I
  RAINBOW
      B
      O
      W
</pre>

A

Rainbow from Heaven

Arched

In colors of interesting beauty,

Nicely shaping itself

Between points

Of our widest,

Wildest and keen imaginations.

Richard L. Allen

```
        A
        W
        E
        D
  WEDDING
        I
        N
        G
```

A **W**edding is *Heavenly* beautiful, all this and more. Its
An **E**ternal *Blessed* union
   A **D**evine communion
     A **D**evoted relationship
      An **I**nternal, exuberant and special togetherness.
       A **N**ever ending love affair and most of all
        A ***G****od **Blessed Matrimony**.*

Poetic & Religiously Beautiful

```
    C
    I
    N
    D
CINDERELLA
    R
    E
    L
    L
    A
```

Cinderella
Our
Beautiful
Lord
And
God,
Cinderella
Of
This
Real
World
And
Life's
Umbrella
When

There's
A
Need
To
Weather
Any
Unbearable
Situation
Situational
Heat
Or
Storm.

Richard L. Allen

                T
                R
                Y
                T
TRY TRY TRY
                Y
                T
                R
                Y
                M
                E

Our Good Lord above
Is waiting with open arms
For us
To Try Him.

Don't just say
We
Or I
Tried,
We
Must continue
To Try Him.

Poetic & Religiously Beautiful

Don't just say
We
Are or I'm
Tired,
We must continue
To Try Him.

Don't just say
Our
Or my
Hands
Are tied,
We must continue
To untiringly,
Untie
Our
Hearts,
Minds,
Tongues
And *Retry Him.*

Richard L. Allen

```
        E
        X
        H
   EXHALTED
        L
        T
        E
        D
```

Christ Our Lord,
The *Glorious*
And *Illustrious*
One.

    The *One*
    And *Only*
    Exaltation
    Of human life.

All
Christians
Exalt
His
Name
And acclaim
Him

As *Supreme*
King
And *Lord*
Over what is
Over what is to be
And
Over what was.

Poetic & Religiously Beautiful

```
    T
    A
    R
TARRIED
    I
    E
    D
```

Those of us whom have happily arrived
On our hands
And knees,
Before *Christ*
Our Lord
And God.
And spirituality cried
Out to *Him*
In prayer,
Thankfulness
And redemption,
Must continue
To tarry
And carry
On,
Out of trust,
Respect
And Love
For the One Above All.

Richard L. Allen

ASCEND ABOVE OUR DESCEND

Ascending to *Heaven*
Should be our foremost and concise
Concern, to begin with and
E
N
D

With, versus

Descending to hell. The primary concern for
Everyone to avoid; also un-necessary and hellish
Smoking is the evil smoke king's foremost,
Cancerous and cigarette/sickarette butt burning
E
N
D

To *Heavenly* and
Healthy in the pink lungs.

Poetic & Religiously Beautiful

HALLELUJAH

Honor our God

And

Lord with our highest, joyful

Laudable praises from our mouths and hearts.

Eagerly entertain all

Levels of His

Unending mercy and the

Joy Of His Love,

As we continue to seek

Him throughout our lives.

Richard L. Allen

ALMIGHTY

Almighty and divine

Love is

Made and began

In *Heaven*, along with a divine toast for *Heaven* bound,

God fearing and faithful believers in *Our Dear Lord*.

His *Heavenly Haven* has

The almighty

Yeast to raise *His* and our *Love* to amazing levels.

SAVED

```
    S
    A
SAVED
    E
    D
```

Saved is to be saved from start to finish.

Saved from a life and world of prolonged evils
Attaching ourselves to the words of *Our Lord* and onto **a**
Vehicle on a trip to *Heaven*, with *Christ* as our nav
Enabling us to enjoy all of *His Blessings*, while
Decidedly entering *The Kingdom of Our Lord and God*.

Richard L. Allen

SABBATH

S
A
B
SABBATH
A
T
H

Saturday or a Sunday
A day to remember to keep *Holy,*
Because it's a special day in remembrance of our many
Blessed days
Amongst
The many other *Blessings Our Heavenly Father*
Has and will bestow upon us.

Thank You Dear Lord

Y
YOU
U
R
S

For You And Yours

Poetic & Religiously Beautiful

SEPULCHRE

S
E
P
U
SEPULCHRE
C
H
R
E

Our
Savior's
ever so resting
place is of the
utmost importance in all of our
lives. Without His
crucifixion we wouldn't
have a chance for Heavenly closure, peace or
rest in any of our
eternal lives.

Richard L. Allen

BELIEVERS

I offer no apology
    For what I believe.
I offer no apologies
    For the Lord I believe in.
I won't become apologetic
    To the non-believers.
I am an apologist
    Of those who believe.
I won't ever apologize
    For my strong *God-fearing* beliefs
Or for the apologists
    Of my beliefs.
I have apologized
    And will continue apologizing
    For failing to believe
    During brief
    Times of grief.

Poetic & Religiously Beautiful

STRAIGHTWAY

Instead of following someone else's narrow
Straight way,
Create a wide
Straight way
Of your own, leaving a wider
And hopefully wiser
Straightway
For many others
To wisely
Follow.

Richard L. Allen

HILLTOPS

Christians
Helping
Others
Struggling
To
Venture
Up
Rocky
And
Cumbersome
Hills,
Will
Eventually
Find
Themselves
Venturing
Near
Or
At
The
Top
Of
The
Same
Hills,
At
The
After
Climb.

DRUG ADDICTS

How can they be committed
To anything worth while
When they're addicted
To things not worth while.
A drug
Or smoking
Addiction
Is a life long affliction.
Leaving some uncommitted
To the things
That mean the most
In their worth while lives.
Further leaving them
Non-committed
To *God*
And their
Families,
Who are foremost
In their
Self indicted
Lives.
It takes a lot of courage
To curtail inner rage
To know when to stand up
Sit down
Speak out
Speak within
Stop
Go
Shut up
And/or shut down
Worthlessness
For the sake of *righteousness*.

HE

Help us to
Endure *Your Beloved Earth* to the end.

His Love

Heaven and
Earth is *Yours, Dear Lord*

He *Is Forever* and
Endearing.

He is the beginning of our hearts, use the
Ears in our

Hearts and
Earth, listen to *Him* and allow

Him to
Enter and guide us from

His
Earth to

His
Eternal Heaven, which is

His
Eternal plan.

Poetic & Religiously Beautiful

POWA

Peace One With Another

Peace be still and real

                                        at the sides of our sister

                                              and brother

Peace be still and honorable

                                                to our father
                                                and mother

Peace be still and forever

                                              with each other

                                                           at

Peace.

Richard L. Allen

      T
      R
TRUTH
      T
      H

TRUTH

The truth
Is always above us
And truly
Ready to surround, and guide us.
The thorough facts in the truth

      r   Its certainty
      u   r
      t   u
      h   t
                              h

Are its honesty
      r   And its reality
      u   r
      t   u
      h   t
                              h

Poetic & Religiously Beautiful

<pre>
    G
  GOD
    D

    G
    O
    D
</pre>

GOD

God is in all that's Good

He is our best
Friend for better
Or worst.
He is the beginning
And ending
Of all Good

He is our Go
To person
In all times of needs,
Despite our not so Good
Deeds.

We must take heed
In all of *His Commandments* and feed
From them as food
For thought,
And acting out our thinking.

Richard L. Allen

LIVE OR DIE

(crossed with LORD vertically through the O)

To live forever
A prepared happy
And *Heavenly*
Life
Or
To forever
Die,
A continuous painful
And hell bound
Death,
Which is our forever
Choice.

He
Above is the beginning
And beginner
Of *Heaven*.

He
Went to the cross
For us to have that choice.

Poetic & Religiously Beautiful

A TRUE LIVING GOD

Our Lord God
Is true
And the truth
In every aspect
Of truism.

He
Is a living
And giving
Lord And God
In every aspect
Of believing
In Him
And all
That is *His*.

Richard L. Allen

OUR
S
A
L
V
SALVATION
T
I
O
N

Our salvation *Above Life,*
Came about To afford us
From *His* The opportunity to live up
Giving up And forever in eternal
Or lying down *Heaven,*
His And to incredibly

Love
The One
Responsible.

Poetic & Religiously Beautiful

VICTORY

Victory for all of us
Was achieved **V** from the
Cross. **I** The cross
With all **C** roads
Leading V I C **T** O R Y to
Heaven. **O** The cross
Is the **R** spot
Where the **Y** victory
March began
And will end in Heaven.

Richard L. Allen

```
        I
        L
        O
   LOVE   LOVE
        V
        E
        Y
        O
        U
```

There's no greater display
Of abundant love
As a result of what *Our
Father*
Did for us.

He's giving us
A choice to live
Happily
Forever
Or
To endure pain
And suffering
Forever.

He's inviting us
To live
In *His* house,
Heaven.

He's
The beginning
And originator
Of the only *Heaven.*

Poetic & Religiously Beautiful

```
      H
      E
   HEART
      R
      T
```

He art
From *His Heart*
Our Holy Father.
He's the ears
In the center
Of our hearts.

He is the beginning
Of *Heaven*
And of every heart.
This earth
Was derived from *His Heart*.

Hear *Him*
From the very top,
Beginning
And true center
Of all of our hearts.

He's The First,
Foremost Father
And the *First*
Heart
Derived from *Father.*

He articulated
Our being
Because of *His Love*
From His Heart.

The End
Is closer than we think

www.ingramcontent.com/pod-product-compliance
Lightning Source LLC
Chambersburg PA
CBHW052044070526
44584CB00018B/2598